"Shinn stands apart among American fusing the political and the personal in almost scary. *Dying City* posits a grievous, very definite familiar war, and it's hard not to relate Mary Tyrone's great remark to the effect that 'the past is present . . . the future too' to Shinn's own sense of the collapsibility of time, as borne out by a structure in which past and present bleed achingly into one another, and give scant hope for the future. Shinn's mournful framework ultimately comes to rest with the damning realization that the war is who we are."

— MATT WOLF, Broadway.com (London)

"*Dying City* is a play about the war that doesn't have to keep telling us it's about the war. Rather, the play homes in on one family's fractures to reflect the larger chaos of the war . . . It confronts us with some essential causes of war: the ways in which flawed, wounded individuals who do not find ways to heal their pain may find themselves inflicting fresh wounds on a more universally devastating scale. So while the title *Dying City* may sound overblown for a two-actor piece set in a single room, by the end of its intense ninety minutes the play feels large enough to have earned the title of *Dying World*."

— LOUISE KENNEDY, *Boston Globe*

"*Dying City* is a taut series of short, intense scenes that build on each other to form a surprising and devastating picture of personal ruin. Shinn reveals a complex web of truths, lies and delusions involving the characters' feelings about the Iraq war and about themselves and one another. *Dying City* is a superb example of the compelling drama that awaits those willing to abandon their television remotes and enlist for the emotional war zone that is live theater at its best."

— ORLA SWIFT, *News & Observer* (North Carolina)

"In *Dying City*, everything seethes with subtext . . . Shinn writes nicely understated menace well; he knows how people play people. *Dying City* is always gripping."

—GILBERT WONG, *Metro Live* (New Zealand)

"*Dying City* has a remarkable reach. It pokes its nose into family dynamics and the puzzles we're left with when people disappear from our lives, even as it probes the consequences of a faraway war for those back home. Shinn is skilled at the betraying pause, and the gaps between words are packed with meanings, unspoken questions and distress. Your thoughts about Shinn's creations just keep piling up."

—MAXIE SZALWINSKA, *Metro* (London)

"*Dying City* is an absorbing drama about grief, power struggles and violence. With war as a backdrop, Shinn fixes his gaze on the tiny, escalating combat between Kelly and Peter, and, with forensic precision, gradually reveals Kelly and Peter's stark, shifting perspectives as they deal with their loss. Shinn's exploration of brutality, deception and the minefield of love is crafted with great economy and restraint."

—BRYCE HALLETT, *Sydney Morning Herald* (Australia)

"*Dying City* is a fragile and slow-boiling study of wartime grief and nonclosure. Silence spotlights Shinn's power as a dramatist, not least of which is his mastery of subtext and the small but eloquent gesture. The drama is mostly quiet and understated, of a work that has been crafted with evident care and intelligence."

—DAVID COTE, *TimeOut New York*

"Since the Twin Towers fell, plays which draw comparison between how we live and how we wage war have been thick on the ground. Few have been as good as this compact and profound two-hander from American playwright Christopher Shinn. The topics covered are varied: war, relationships, acting. But at the heart of every conversation is violence—how it infects our lives and separates us."

—KIERON QUIRKE, *Evening Standard* (London)

"*Dying City* is a remarkable tale of loss. It is personal, intimate even, yet its themes could not be more all-encompassing and its emotional impact more affecting. In this subtle and revealing play, Shinn is able to take the political and humanize it, transforming the stuff of daily news stories into a devastating statement on the unforeseen and often hidden consequences of war."

—MICHAEL KUCHWARA, Associated Press

"Shinn is a gifted dramatist . . . Most political plays go for the punch of anger, but in *Dying City*, an achingly compassionate play, Shinn's achievement is to have written a drama of rare delicacy in which politics are not in the character's mouths, but in their circumstances and lives."

—DAVID BENEDICT, *Variety*

DYING CITY

DYING CITY

CHRISTOPHER SHINN

THEATRE COMMUNICATIONS GROUP
NEW YORK
2008

This publication is made possible in part with public funds from the New York State Council on the Arts, a State Agency.

TCG books are exclusively distributed to the book trade by Consortium Book Sales and Distribution.

LIBRARY OF CONGRESS CATALOGING-IN-PUBLICATION DATA
Shinn, Christopher.
Dying city / by Christopher Shinn.—1st ed.
p. cm.
Includes bibliographical references and index.
ISBN 978-1-55936-329-7 (alk. paper)
1. War widows—Drama. 2. Brothers—Drama. 3. Iraq War, 2003—
Psychological aspects—Drama. 4. New York (N.Y.)—Drama. I. Title.
PS3569.H498D95   2008
812'54—dc22   2008017278

Book design and composition by Lisa Govan
Cover design by Mark Melnick
Cover photograph by Nikola Tamindzic

First Edition, August 2008

For E & L

ACKNOWLEDGMENTS

For their contributions to the development of this script, I owe profound thanks to Emily Bergl, André Bishop, Sian Brooke, Rebecca Brooksher, Walter A. Davis, Ben Kessler, George Lane, James Macdonald, Luke Macfarlane, Ian Rickson, Pablo Schreiber, Andrew Scott, Sarah Stern, David Turner and Graham Whybrow.

DYING CITY

PRODUCTION HISTORY

In May 2006, *Dying City* received its world premiere by The English Stage Company at the Royal Court Theatre in London. It was directed by James Macdonald; design and lighting were by Peter Mumford. The cast included:

KELLY	Sian Brooke
CRAIG/PETER	Andrew Scott

In March 2007, *Dying City* received its U.S. premiere at Lincoln Center Theater (André Bishop, Artistic Director; Bernard Gersten, Executive Producer) in New York. It was directed by James Macdonald; sets and costumes were by Anthony Ward, lighting was by Pat Collins, sound was by Aural Fixation; the stage manager was Roy Harris. The cast included:

KELLY	Rebecca Brooksher
CRAIG/PETER	Pablo Schreiber

CHARACTERS

Kelly, late twenties
Craig, late twenties
Peter, late twenties

Craig and Peter are identical twins and played by the same actor.

TIME

The play takes place in July 2005 and January 2004.

NOTE

No interval; blackouts should be avoided; sound between scenes should not be over-designed. The play takes place in Kelly's apartment: a combined living room/kitchen is visible; doors lead to a bathroom and bedroom off. I imagine a design that lives in naturalism but suggests something beyond it. I've kept stage directions to a minimum, omitting obvious actions, in an attempt to avoid clutter.

Dialogue in the play often overlaps. A slash in the text (/) indicates where the character who speaks next begins.

A lie sweet in the mouth
is sour in the stomach.

—Aeschylus, *The Oresteia*
Translated by Ted Hughes

1.

Night. Kelly sorts through books. A cardboard box sits next to the couch. TV plays Law and Order. *A bedsheet and pillow are scrunched up in the corner of the couch.*
  The buzzer buzzes.

                                KELLY
Hello?

                             PETER'S VOICE
Hi—it's Peter!

(Pause.)

                                KELLY
Hi!

                             PETER'S VOICE
I tried calling . . .

(Pause.)

KELLY

Come up!

(Pause. Kelly throws the bedsheet over the box. Peter knocks.)

Hi! Peter . . .

PETER

Hi Kelly—sorry!

KELLY

—Come in.

PETER

You're unlisted now!

KELLY

I am . . .

PETER

I tried calling your land line, and then I tried your cell—I was wondering, I thought maybe it was a *work* thing, maybe one of your clients got your numbers or something and you / had to change—

KELLY

It's—yeah, it's. —I've been meaning to call you and—it's—I just haven't. I've been so / busy—

PETER

Oh, no, of course—

KELLY

I wanted to make sure I had the, that I had enough—energy, mental space, before I called . . .

PETER

Did you, I wasn't—did you get my letter?

6

KELLY

—I did.

PETER

I was wondering, I wasn't sure if I had the right address—

KELLY

I did. Yeah, and I just—I've been *meaning* to call—

PETER

No—of *course*.

KELLY

So . . .

(Pause.)

Well—sit down, please! I'll make some tea.

PETER

Oh, tea would be lovely.

KELLY

Were you—in the neighborhood or—you're in town visiting? . . .

PETER

—I know, barging in like this, I have to apologize.

KELLY

Well—I don't have a phone.

PETER

(Laughs) Right. No, I didn't plan on—tonight—it's actually a bit of a *drama* actually.

KELLY

Oh?

(Pause.)

PETER

I'm sorry, is everything—did I, is it a bad—a bad / time or—

KELLY

No. No.

PETER

I just . . .

(Pause.)

KELLY

You know, honestly—when they come to tell you—

(Pause.)

When they came to tell me about Craig, they just showed up—
they just / show up, no warning, they don't call or—

PETER

Oh God. Oh Kelly, I'm so sorry. I'm so *stupid*.

KELLY

So I was just—a memory . . .

PETER

Of *course*.

KELLY

. . . of the buzzer—I'm fine.

PETER

God, I'm a total idiot.

KELLY

I'm fine.

PETER

And it's just about a year, right?

KELLY

Last week. Yeah.

PETER

Last *week*. Huh. I've been—the date was sort of floating around in my head but I've been kind of distracted because of these other . . . I've been thinking a lot about the *funeral* actually.

KELLY

Uh-huh?

PETER

Just how weird it was.

KELLY

Yeah.

PETER

No one really talking.

KELLY

Mm. No one knew what to *say*.

PETER

About?

KELLY

Just—you know, the shock. Everyone was in shock.

PETER

Okay. I thought you meant—knew what to say, like, weren't sure what to say because it seemed like maybe what happened wasn't what the military was saying.

KELLY

Oh.

PETER

Did you feel that at all? I don't know, maybe I'm crazy, but I felt that underneath a little, that people kind of thought it wasn't an accident maybe, and that's why everyone was so quiet.

KELLY

Well. The way it was told to us—so many of his men saw it happen . . .

PETER

Yeah—I guess I thought maybe, because everyone there knew that Dad taught us, from the time we were little, how to shoot, how to handle weapons, that maybe some people didn't believe the story.

KELLY

Right. Well, the investigation was still going on at that point, it wasn't official, so some people might have felt that.

PETER

Yeah. And maybe it's a gun culture thing, we grew up around guns, you didn't, so it's something I would feel more than you . . . —*Target* practice, I just . . . Craig would always write about how careful he was with his weapon—I still can't picture it.

KELLY

It's a hard thing to picture.

(Pause.)

PETER

Another thing that sucked was I could only be there for one *day*, remember? I had to fly back and do those stupid reshoots on my movie. The whole thing was so, it's like this *blur*—dealing with Mom, two years after Dad—and, like, the whole *gay* thing, do these people know, or not, and no one *talking* to me—except you.

KELLY

—How is your mom?

PETER

Oh, the same. I don't know what it will take to pierce that woman's heart, but . . .

(Pause.)

KELLY

Well—I'm glad you're here. However. It's great to see you.

PETER

A bit weird maybe?

KELLY

Weird—a little. How you look.

PETER

Yeah, I always think of that . . . A relief, though, too.

KELLY

Uh-huh? . . .

PETER

That's how *I* feel. Even though it's hard. To finally see you again. —Not since the funeral, God! Even *spoken*!

KELLY

Time. I can't believe so much time has passed—

PETER

It feels like yesterday, right? —I wonder if the anniversary— because I wasn't aware of the exact date—if that had anything to do with what happened tonight.

KELLY

—What happened?

PETER

I . . . —I did something sort of shocking.

(Pause.)

I'm sorry.

KELLY

What?

PETER

I know I've already said this, but I can't believe I just showed up like this. Because—we talked, at the funeral, about what it was *like* for you when they just showed up and buzzed—and here I go do the exact same thing!

KELLY

—You didn't have my number, what other way could you have gotten in / touch?

PETER

I know, but still . . .

KELLY

It's fine. Really. Forget about it.

(Pause. Peter smiles.)

PETER

Oh, all right, if you *insist* . . .

(Kelly smiles.)

Was it—is everything okay, I mean . . . ?

KELLY

With . . . ?

PETER

Did you have to change your numbers because of a client, did something happen?

KELLY

—Oh.

PETER

I always worried something *stalkery* would happen to you, you're so beautiful.

KELLY

—Oh!

PETER

I'm serious! Therapy, you know, two people alone in a room, it's very sexy! —Not that I've ever *done* it. In my fantasies—"the handsome doctor . . ."

KELLY

—You take sugar, right? I only have whole milk—

PETER

Plain is fine.

KELLY

Plain?

PETER

Yes—I'm playing this *assassin* in this movie I have coming up, I'm supposed to be getting in shape—I have this *trainer* . . .

KELLY

He's tough?

PETER

She—the guy trainers I've had, it's weird, I think they've all been jealous of me—my manager thinks it's because I'm so handsome. —But yes, she is tough.—

KELLY

—It's funny, you know, you say what you imagine therapy is like—when I first started I thought I'd get to hear people talk about sex, their sex lives? But it's food. People want to talk about eating—their *body* image, their *eating* habits—

PETER

That's so pathetic.

KELLY

It's really what people are obsessed with.

PETER

Yeah, because nobody fucks anymore, they just eat like pigs instead!

(Pause.)

KELLY

I don't know about that. Viagra's still pretty popular . . .

PETER

That's true I guess . . . —Right! There's your problem—the people who would have gone to therapy and talked about sex are all just popping Viagra instead!

KELLY

Huh . . .

PETER

—Oh, but, what about fucked-her-so-hard-she? *He* wanted to talk about sex.

(A moment. Then:)

KELLY

—What?

PETER

It just came into my head, your client—we talked about him on Craig's last night. —That was what we called him, right? Fucked-her-so- / hard-she?

KELLY

—Wow, you remember that?

PETER

We talked about him half the night, how could I forget?! Coming up with our little theories about him—*Tim* thought he should go on Prozac, of course.

KELLY

—How *is* Tim? Nice to hear his name . . .

PETER

Tim's well, he's well. Just went back to Los Angeles, yesterday actually—school's starting in a month, month and a half, so . . .

KELLY

You guys were here? . . .

PETER

He just came to visit—I've been here—I'm doing a play? . . .

KELLY

—*That's* right.

PETER

Long Day's Journey into Night—

KELLY

Of course—in the letter you—yes.

PETER

So . . . he was out for the opening in April, then came back after school got out . . . I've been here since *February*, God.

KELLY

—I remember now. So you've been here a while!

PETER

Yeah, it has been . . .

KELLY

And Tim went back to get ready for school?

PETER

Another year of figuring out how to get inner-city eighth graders interested in *Romeo and Juliet*. Hopeless . . .

KELLY

—You should go to his class, do a dramatic reading.

PETER

I suggested that! But he has this idea that it would be "disruptive." Since I'm "famous."

KELLY

I can see that.

PETER

Oh, please, my movie *tanked*. Did you see it?

KELLY

You know—I usually wait for the / DVD—

PETER

Oh God, it was *so* stinky—oh!

KELLY

Really? I've always been curious about that process—because I remember you said it was a good script. So how does it become a bad / movie?

PETER

Right—I was just about to start shooting, on Craig's last night, we talked about it . . . —Why are we—who cares about my career, how boring!

KELLY

It's not boring to *me*—

PETER

To me it's like the least interesting—I guess we all get bored talking about work. Of course *I* want to know about fucked-her-so-hard-she, you probably find talking about *that* boring.

KELLY

—I can't believe you remember that. You have such / a good—

PETER

We had such an interesting debate on how you should handle him! *I* thought he was lying just to sound interesting, Tim thought he was self-medicating—Craig didn't think he was *lying*, just that he wanted to torture you—and didn't actually want to get better.

KELLY

Craig the expert—

PETER

Fucked-her-so-hard-she . . . What happened with him, how did things turn / out?

KELLY

—I have to say, I hated that nickname Craig gave him. It was so crass.

PETER

But—wasn't that how the guy himself—didn't he, say, like—

KELLY

It was how he would phrase his conquests—

PETER

Which is all he ever would talk about, right? And he would always use the same phrase: "I fucked her so hard she came six times."

KELLY

Yes—

PETER

"I fucked her so hard she started crying,"—"I fucked her so hard she—woke up my ninety-year-old-hearing-impaired neighbor"—

KELLY

Well—he didn't go *that* far. —You know, it slipped my mind a second ago—but I have to say—I read a number of just incredible reviews for the play. You opened in April you said?

(Peter makes "masturbation" motion.)

What.

PETER

—It's a terrible production.

KELLY

No.

(Peter nods.)

I had made a plan to come and just never got around / to it—

PETER

You're not missing anything.

KELLY

What's—wrong with it?

PETER

It's not true.

(Pause.)

KELLY

I'm sorry to hear that.

PETER

Yeah. "Oh well!" *(Smiles)* The "drama" is actually—I'm still kind of in shock I think—but the drama is that I walked offstage tonight—in the middle of the show.

(Pause.)

KELLY

—Oh.

PETER

Yeah.

KELLY

I was going to—because I remember it being a pretty long / play—

PETER

Yeah.

(Pause.)

KELLY

—Is your tea okay? . . .

PETER

No, it's because there isn't any sugar. I don't want to drink it.

KELLY

Oh—would you like / some—

PETER

No—I can't.

(Pause.)

Yeah. Right before the intermission—my dad is calling me from offstage, "Come on, Edmund!" I make my exit and there he is— Tyrone, John Conrad—you know him, right? Very big / man—

KELLY

Mm-hmm—

PETER

So he sort of beckons me over, like, with this look on his face like he has a joke to tell me, or some little piece of gossip. So I go over, I lean into him, he grabs my shoulder and whispers into my ear, "I have a piece of advice for you." He says, "You're never—"

(Pause.)

He says, "You're never going to be a good actor till you stop sucking cock."

KELLY

—Oh.

PETER

Applause, act's over, I'm standing there *stunned,* he's looking at me and smiling this, this *smile,* and then he takes me, it's sort of like he's shoving me aside, but, like, *really* hard—

KELLY

Oh, Peter.

PETER

—I thought about going to the stage manager, telling her what happened, but John is the star, and no one else *saw* so he can just *lie* and—you know, in rehearsals, with John, and Scott, the director—I talked about *Dad* dying of leukemia, I talked about *Craig* dying in Iraq, I—and so I'm in my dressing room at this point, all alone, imagining having to go back out there with this man and pour my heart out to him and . . . —I looked in the mirror and I just grabbed my stuff and left.

(Pause.)

KELLY

You did the right thing.

PETER

I didn't, though— I should have gone to the stage manager. I fucked up the whole second half of the / show.

KELLY

You can do all the formal stuff tomorrow—I'm sure you have an understudy.

PETER

Drew. He like does coke and gets escorts, I don't even think he knows the lines.

KELLY

Well. You'll straighten it out tomorrow.

(Pause.)

PETER

Then the *other* thing is—I broke up with Tim last night.

KELLY

You broke up with / Tim?

(Peter's mobile phone rings, he checks it.)

PETER

I should . . .

(Kelly nods. Peter gestures toward the bedroom. Kelly nods again. Peter answers the phone as he moves into the bedroom, off . . .)

2.

Night. Kelly cleans up. Craig comes out of the bedroom, helps.

CRAIG

He's wasted.

KELLY

He's wasted? He didn't drink that much.

CRAIG

He's passed out . . .

KELLY

He just had two cups of coffee!

CRAIG

Yeah, with enough sugar to light up a room full of third graders.

KELLY

Well he *can't* be passed out for long.

CRAIG

It's ridiculous at his age. Ever since he was little—used to pour sugar on top of his Frosted Flakes, drove Dad crazy—

KELLY

Ohhh.

CRAIG

What.

KELLY

I bet he took a Xanax.

CRAIG

A Xanax?

KELLY

You were in the bathroom. Tim had Xanax for the plane, he hates flying.

CRAIG

What happened when I was in the bathroom?

KELLY

We were talking about Black Hawks—

CRAIG

Yeah—

KELLY

You got up to pee, and Tim said he couldn't imagine doing what you did because he couldn't even fly on a *commercial* plane without taking a Xanax. Then he took a bottle out of his pocket and shook it for effect.

CRAIG

"Shook it for effect"?

KELLY

It was cute.

CRAIG

So Peter took one?

KELLY

Not at the table—I'm just guessing—at some point.

CRAIG

But they're not prescribed to him.

(Pause.)

KELLY

Well . . .

CRAIG

That's a powerful drug! He's not a doctor. I bet this shit flows in Hollywood / like fucking—

KELLY

One Xanax, I mean . . .

CRAIG

Yeah, one Xanax and he's so fucked-up he can't even talk, he's in there *drooling.*

(Pause.)

KELLY

So maybe he took two.

CRAIG

—Why are you being flip? You're against these drugs.

KELLY

In my *work*—when people medicate so they don't have to look at their problems—not as a once-in-a-while / thing.

CRAIG

I'm going to Fort Benning in the morning and now I can't even say good-bye to him!

(Pause.)

KELLY

I'm sorry. How are you feeling?

CRAIG

A little agitated. I mean I'm *fine* . . . How are you?

KELLY

All things considered . . .

CRAIG

Yeah?

(Pause.)

I guess it was a nice night.

KELLY

It was.

CRAIG

He was nervous, but—I thought he'd be much worse.

KELLY

Peter or Tim?

CRAIG

Peter.

KELLY

You really do overestimate his attachment to you.

CRAIG

I know you think that—

KELLY

I think you need to be on the outside to see it. He's not seven anymore, copying the way you walk and talk. Look at when we were talking about Iraq—we really got into it!

CRAIG

(A realization) I think *I* was more nervous than I expected.

KELLY

Really? You didn't seem nervous to me.

CRAIG

No?

KELLY

At most I would say—you were a little more "animated" than usual.

CRAIG

I thought it got most intense when we were talking about his career. That's where I felt maybe I went too far.

KELLY

—It's amazing, isn't it? Peter's gonna be a movie star! He's gonna be rich!

CRAIG

That movie sounded so fucking offensive.

KELLY

Yeah, but I agree with Peter, within the confines of what they / make today—

CRAIG

That's the thing. You start telling yourself / that—

KELLY

—But think why we don't have any Brandos or James Deans anymore—they're not, it's all so corporate-controlled, nobody's writing parts that a Brando or a—imagine Marlon Brando doing *Titanic*. James Dean in *Lord of the Rings*, I mean—

CRAIG

But I'm talking about—yes, all the capitalist, corporate, I know Peter's not going to be in *Rebel without a Cause* his first movie out—but I'm talking about Peter saying he thought the movie was *good*. *That's* what makes / me—

KELLY

Within the *confines* of what they produce today.

CRAIG

But that's exactly what—why can't he just say, "It's a bad movie, it's a piece of shit, but I have to start somewhere." What does that mean, "good within the confines"? You could say that about any movie, basically. Peter's too smart to start thinking that / way—

KELLY

Well, we don't know anything about the movie.

CRAIG

Yeah, but from what he said—"special forces," "covert operations"—come on. I mean, do the movie, fine, but don't trick yourself about what it is.

(Pause.)

KELLY

I think it was a good night.

CRAIG

Yeah . . . yeah. Why not. Let's call it a good night.

KELLY

It was.

CRAIG

Just . . . I wanted to say good-bye in a more formal way.

KELLY

—So wake him up.

CRAIG

Nah, moment's gone.

(Pause.)

KELLY

—You brought up fucked-her-so-hard-she, that threw me for a loop.

CRAIG

Oh God—it just came out . . .

KELLY

Out of *nowhere* . . .

CRAIG

I was thinking out loud. —I was pretty drunk there, till you put the coffee on.

KELLY

Why were you thinking about *him*?

CRAIG

Just—I don't know, you're seeing him in the morning . . .

KELLY

So?

CRAIG

Just—crossed my mind

(Pause.)

KELLY

I forgot for a second.

CRAIG

What?

KELLY

Morning . . .

(Pause.)

CRAIG

—At least it got Tim talking, finally.

KELLY

What?

CRAIG

Fucked-her-so-hard-she. Tim thought he was "clinically depressed."

KELLY

He was very articulate, I thought.

CRAIG

No, yeah—I liked him. Did you like him?

KELLY

Oh, definitely! They're great together.

CRAIG

Yeah . . . A little quiet . . .

KELLY

I'm sure he was *nervous*—meeting his boyfriend's identical *twin*—

CRAIG

No, I know . . . —You didn't think anything was off with him?

KELLY

No, not at all.

CRAIG

I don't know, I had this little nagging, like—just this feeling that something was off. Like—like I couldn't picture them fucking.

KELLY

—Craig!

CRAIG

Just, the vibe wasn't—whatever, he's better than The Psychopath.

KELLY

Oh, Craig.

CRAIG

I know you have a soft spot for him—

KELLY

I actually don't—but Adam was not a psychopath. He had *quirks,* he had *issues*—

CRAIG

"Quirks"?

KELLY

Whatever you want to call them. His personality was *affected* by the abuse he suffered. That doesn't make / him a—

CRAIG

—The abuse he *claimed* to have suffered.

KELLY

Well, we don't know if he did or not.

CRAIG

Wait—I thought you told Peter it never happened, the abuse. After Adam dumped him.

KELLY

I told Peter it was *possible* it never happened. I / can't—

CRAIG

That's not what he told me—he told me you told him you thought Adam made it up.

KELLY

Well . . . that's not what I said.

CRAIG

So you think it's possible that Adam's older brother forced him to give blow jobs to all the boys in the neighborhood, every day after school for two years, when he was six years / old—

KELLY

I think it's unlikely. But what I told Peter is that the memories could be an elaboration of something *less* severe that *did* happen. Or a fantasy that he got mixed up with reality because he was so young at the time / he—

CRAIG

—Or a lie. Meant to make Peter feel guilty, so he'd never dump Adam.

KELLY

Or that. —The point is, even if it isn't in any way *literally* true, the fact that Adam goes around telling people that this happened means he feels that something traumatic *did* happen to him when he was a boy, and that this "story" is the only way he has of communicating that trauma. You know, his parents were clearly very / disturbed—

CRAIG

See—this is what worries me about you. You're the same way with fucked-her-so-hard-she, you're so passive, or finding / ways to—

KELLY

—Can you stop calling him that now?

CRAIG

—What?

KELLY

It was one thing when it was just between us, but—he's a human being.

CRAIG

I'm just saying—if you know someone is manipulating you, then you should tell them, "Look, I know what you're doing, stop it."

KELLY

Even if he *were* manipulating me—if I said that, he would never come back to therapy!

CRAIG

So what! At least this way he would know, he would have to walk around knowing that someone knew the truth!

KELLY

The purpose of therapy is to help someone change, not just / face the truth—

CRAIG

That's what I'm saying—people like that don't want to change, they just want to see what they can get away with—

KELLY

—Stop.

(Pause.)

This always happens when we talk seriously about my work.

CRAIG

We don't talk seriously about your work.

KELLY

Exactly, / because

CRAIG

Okay—

KELLY

you treat me like I'm this ridiculous person. Which does not make me feel *good,* or *loved,* / or—

CRAIG

Okay—

KELLY

Every time we talk about therapy or money, you get revved up, you / start getting—

CRAIG

Money?

KELLY

Yes—like tonight, when Tim started talking about his upbringing, you did the exact same thing you used to do when Adam would talk about growing up on the Upper East Side, or going to Horace / Mann—

CRAIG

Adam— / no—

KELLY

You turned off. You did. I think *that's* what was "off" to you about Tim—that he comes from money. It's why you have problems with my *dad*, it's why *therapy* / bothers you—

CRAIG

Problems with your dad?

KELLY

—When you criticize his lifestyle, his / attitude—

CRAIG

My problem with your dad is that he didn't love you. And the thing that was off to me about Tim—was that they didn't leave together.

(Pause.)

KELLY

I did think that was weird.

(Pause.)

Maybe Peter wanted to say good-bye to you alone.

CRAIG

Then why did he—I don't know, something didn't feel right.

KELLY

I'm sure that's it.

(Pause.)

CRAIG

—I also thought it was weird how much his phone kept ringing. Agents and managers call so late? How many times do they need to call?

(Pause.)

                    KELLY

Speaking of late . . .

(Pause.)

                    CRAIG

Yeah . . .

(Pause.)

—Okay. Do up the couch, I'll move Peter out / here—

                    KELLY

—What?

                    CRAIG

What?

                    KELLY

He's *staying*?

                    CRAIG

On the couch . . .

                    KELLY

Craig—I said, if he comes is this going to turn into an all-night thing? You said / no—

                    CRAIG

Kelly, he can't even—

                    KELLY

You said no. *Craig*—

                    CRAIG

Okay—

(Pause.)

Okay. I'll call him a car.

(Pause.)

                         KELLY
Thank you.

(Pause. Craig kisses Kelly. He goes into the bedroom, off.)

3.

Kelly watches TV. Peter comes out of the bedroom.

PETER

You painted!

KELLY

Oh—yeah.

PETER

White!

KELLY

Brighten things up . . .

PETER

It looks good. —I'm interrupting your *Law and Order*.

KELLY

Oh, I can watch it whenever.

PETER

TiVo?

KELLY

Yeah. I programmed it to record *Law and Order* whenever it's on—an endless / stream—

PETER

I see mine rerun all the time, it's so humiliating.

KELLY

You're kidding! Why have I never seen it?

PETER

Skater pothead: "Wha? Naw, man, I wasn't in the park that night."

KELLY

Very good!

PETER

(Sitting) Please—the casting director just wanted to fuck me. I told him I couldn't skate, he said, "Oh, it's okay, there's not much skating"—they send me the shooting script, of course I'm on a skateboard in *every* scene.

KELLY

I used to not like *Law and Order*, but then it really started to grow on me.

PETER

Oh yeah?

KELLY

I have this theory about / it—

PETER

—When did you start watching all this TV, I don't remember you being a big TV person.

KELLY

Yeah, I never was before.

PETER

Was it after Craig died?

(Pause.)

KELLY

Maybe—when I couldn't sleep I'd watch TV, I'd / watch—

PETER

I had trouble sleeping—

KELLY

these shows—

PETER

The worst time for me was actually *months* after—when the official report came out that said it was an accident. After that I just couldn't sleep for some reason.

KELLY

Yeah, the grief comes at different times, it's so unpredictable. —But I came up with this theory—would you like to hear / it?

PETER

—Oh, definitely!

KELLY

Well, I realized that all these shows, all the *Law and Orders* and all the rip-offs, have the same exact structure: someone dies, and a whole team of specialists springs up to figure out how to solve the mystery of the person's death.

PETER

Right?

KELLY

Which I think is a fantasy people have—that they won't be for-
gotten. That their death won't just be accepted and mourned,
but that an entire *community* will come together, all these special people—lawyers and scientists and forensics experts, judges,
detectives—who are devoted, who will not stop until the mystery of the death is solved. And therefore symbolically reversed.

PETER

—Wow!

KELLY

Only took me six thousand episodes to figure it out.

PETER

Good use of *insomnia* . . . —It's weird with me, lately—I've been
sleeping fine, but then out of nowhere, doing the play, like—like
the other night. I had this fantasy, this image almost, of a Black
Hawk helicopter crashing through the ceiling of the theater.

KELLY

—While you were onstage?

PETER

At the curtain call—and curtain calls have always been kind of
weird for me, I sort of forget who I am—am I me, or am I the
character? But lately, it's like—I feel like *Craig* in the curtain call.
And I thought—well, it makes sense, that's how I started acting,
when I was little, I would pretend that I was him . . . So maybe
it's a delayed grief reaction, like?

KELLY

—It may be . . .

PETER

Tim thinks I have post-traumatic stress disorder, keeps bugging
me to see his shrink. But I'm like, no—if this is grief, these

"moments"—then I should feel it, right? I don't want to medicate my grief away . . .

KELLY

I'm not a psychiatrist. But I think Tim is right, it does sound like you should see one.

PETER

Really, you think? Huh. That surprises me. I'll think about it then . . .

(Pause.)

—I'm sorry—I feel a little silly asking this, but—are you moving?

(Pause.)

KELLY

You mean—all the boxes—

PETER

Not that you wouldn't *tell* me, I / just—

KELLY

I felt like my life had a lot of clutter, that's all.

PETER

Oh, you're putting some things—

KELLY

In storage, clearing space . . .

PETER

. . . painting . . .

KELLY

So . . .

PETER

That's good . . . —Hey, you know, I know I mentioned to you—
I don't know if you remember—at the funeral? I mentioned
Craig's emails? From Iraq?

KELLY

Yeah—I remember your mentioning them . . .

PETER

I just realized, I actually have them with me.

(Pause.)

KELLY

Uh-huh?

PETER

I keep them at the theater, I read them before shows, and I just
grabbed them before I left tonight. Sort of instinctively . . .

KELLY

Right . . .

PETER

I know—I remember at the funeral your telling me you and
Craig didn't email while he was over there, you just talked on
the phone—something about the distance . . .

KELLY

Email felt weird to me—not intimate.

PETER

Hearing his voice . . .

KELLY

Felt more—

PETER

Right, yeah. But it must—do you ever—now that he's gone, do you ever wish you had anything down on paper, that you could look at, or . . . ?

KELLY

I have other things . . .

PETER

Yeah . . . I guess, too, you were used to distance. I mean—in a way it must seem like he might even be coming back. It's only been a year. He was active duty four years after you guys finished Harvard, that's such a long time to be away from each other—

KELLY

—Well, but I always knew that that would be over some day. There was a very definite timetable when he would be done. Plus he wasn't fighting. So it was always in the background that he'd be coming back . . . which—isn't the case anymore.

PETER

Right—and you were in grad school, and becoming a therapist, so you were also really busy then, you weren't as settled as you are now . . .

KELLY

Exactly.

PETER

I remember when he got called up again, I thought—because he had done his four years, it's like—I knew you go on Inactive Ready Reserves after, but I just assumed he was done. Starting his life finally, writing his dissertation . . . —He never complained, though—wouldn't apply for a deferment . . .

KELLY

He felt a lot of loyalty to the Army—ROTC paid for school. He couldn't have gone to Harvard without it.

PETER

Well, he also believed in the war. There was that also.

(Pause.)

I think it's so sad he never finished his Ph.D. Do you still have all his Faulkner research?

KELLY

I sent it to your mom.

PETER

Really? She never told me that. Typical. God, for a woman who wanted both her sons to get out of the Midwest, she's never stopped resenting us for it. She hasn't come to see my / *play*—

KELLY

—You think it's that?

PETER

What?

KELLY

You think she resents you because you left your—

PETER

Oh, the social class thing, definitely, anything to do with being *educated, cultured,* makes her—I think that was a big reason she didn't—not that she didn't, doesn't *like* you, / but—

KELLY

But isn't it also—very generally, that she resents that her life didn't turn out the way she planned, her husband dying, her son—I mean, she pushed you and Craig very hard in school, didn't she? So you could / get out of—

PETER

Oh, and took us to theater, and took us to museums—but she didn't want us to be cultured so much as she just wanted us to be able to get away from dad. When he got back from Vietnam I think she knew something was—even from pictures you can tell. But she wasn't going to leave him, they had us—so she pushed us to excel, go away to school . . . but once we *did* that— she resented / us.

KELLY

I see. I thought maybe she hadn't told you about the dissertation because it reminds her of everything—that hasn't turned out right.

(Pause.)

PETER

He was such a good writer. These emails—they could be published. I've thought about maybe trying to make them into a one-man show. I don't know if I'd play him. I guess it would make the most sense for me to, but—feels a little—also—they're so intimate, I don't know if I'd want to share them with people. I haven't shown them to anyone.

(Pause.)

I'd—love to share them with you if you . . .

KELLY

Oh. That's . . . you know, I just don't think I'm ready.

(Pause.)

PETER

I understand.

(Pause.)

You can really see in them how much he learned from you, I think . . . just, his emotions and . . . it's hard because, you didn't know him before you met him obviously, but—the way he blossomed with you—especially after you got married . . . God, it's just about three years, right?

KELLY

Just about. September . . .

PETER

Wow. I remember when you guys finally got engaged, him calling me up to tell me—God, I was so happy. Because I was getting, I was definitely, like, Let's hurry it up here!

KELLY

We had always talked about it—he just wanted to wait till he was done with active duty.

PETER

—I also think Dad getting sick definitely—gave him some perspective . . . And 9/11 . . .

(Pause.)

KELLY

—Was that your director who called before? Is / everything—

PETER

—No, I haven't called him back yet, he just left me a voice mail— I was talking to Tim, actually. He's emailing me all this information on PTSD, so . . .

(Pause.)

KELLY

I owe you an apology, Peter.

PETER

—Uh-huh?

KELLY

I know how important it was to you that I stay in touch. I told you at the funeral that I would—and I didn't.

PETER

Oh, thank you . . . no, definitely, I mean—I'd be lying if I said . . . —Part of me, you know, definitely did the play hoping being in the same city would make us . . . you know, even if it meant going away from Tim, and pissing off my agents . . . make us close again.

(Pause.)

KELLY

Your letter really—it really did touch me. I should have responded.

PETER

. . . I knew it was a really big thing I was proposing, so I kind of—I expected you to say, "No," or at least—that you'd need time to think about it . . . —But—yeah, you know? I asked you to have a *baby*, I mean, *some* kind of acknowledgment—

KELLY

I know.

(Pause.)

PETER

—I hate to do this, but I should call Scott back before it gets too late, is that okay?

KELLY

—Sure.

PETER

Thanks.

(Peter takes out his mobile phone and goes back into the bed-room.)

4.

Craig comes out of the bedroom.

KELLY

Hey.

CRAIG

So, I don't think Peter's gonna make it home tonight.

(Pause.)

KELLY

Why not?

CRAIG

I've been trying to get him up for fifteen / minutes—

KELLY

Craig—

CRAIG

I don't know what else to / do.

KELLY

Wake him up.

(Pause.)

Call a car, I'll help you get / him—

CRAIG

—What's the big deal if he just crashes on the couch?

KELLY

I don't want him here.

(Pause.)

CRAIG

You don't want him / here.

KELLY

I don't want him / here.

CRAIG

Why don't you / want him—

KELLY

—All right, what's happening.

(Pause.)

CRAIG

What.

KELLY

Something is happening—

CRAIG

So say it then, what.

KELLY

You don't want to be alone with me.

(Pause.)

CRAIG

That's not true, Kelly. I'm going to *Iraq,* my brother / is—

KELLY

You're going to *Georgia.*

CRAIG

—I'm going to Georgia, and then I'm going to Iraq. What, you think I'm being dramatic?

KELLY

Yes, I do.

CRAIG

—Look, he's not—I don't feel right just throwing him in a car—

KELLY

Why not?

CRAIG

Because I think—he's scared, and I don't think he should have to wake up alone in the morning / like I—

KELLY

—You keep saying he's scared—we talked about the war half the night, he didn't sound scared at all. He sounded very confident—

CRAIG

We were talking about politics, not me leaving.

KELLY

—But if he was so scared, I really don't think he would have been able to disagree with you the way he / did.

CRAIG

That's not even—he was just putting on a show for Tim.

(Pause.)

KELLY

—What?

CRAIG

Tim's against the war, so—whatever, the point is, whatever he said / when we were—

KELLY

No, what do you mean, "putting on a show"?

CRAIG

Tim's—that's actually not how Peter feels, Peter is not "against" the war, he was just saying that for Tim's sake.

KELLY

What? . . .

CRAIG

He—Peter told me that because *Tim* marches against the war, and because all their *friends* are against it, it's just easier for him to keep quiet about how he really feels.

KELLY

So—everything he was saying—was / just—

CRAIG

—His feelings are complicated. He's against the administration, but the actual war he thinks is worth fighting. Tim doesn't feel that way, *obviously*, / so—

KELLY

Wait—is *that* what this is about?

CRAIG

What.

KELLY

Are you acting this way because I agreed with Tim?

(Pause.)

CRAIG

Acting what way.

KELLY

Not wanting to be alone with me—

CRAIG

Kelly, I *do* want to be alone with / you—

KELLY

I could tell you were getting pissed, I just thought it was something to do with Tim. —Is that why you were so pissed off? Because I was / saying that—

CRAIG

—We *have* never really talked about the war in the terms we did tonight.

KELLY

—Yes we have.

CRAIG

—*I* recall your saying to me that it would be good for Saddam to be out of power—when the war started. You disagreed with how we got into it, but you felt the Iraqis / would benefit—

KELLY

—What?

CRAIG

When we watched Tony Blair with Bush, remember? You said how articulate he was—

KELLY

Craig, I said it was a *fake* war that they were *lying* about to get us into—

CRAIG

You don't remember when we watched Blair?

KELLY

I was—*theoretically*, we were talking about human rights in *general*—

CRAIG

And I remember you more or less agreeing with me.

KELLY

I was sympathetic—in the *abstract*—to the "idea" of human rights, I mean, what, did you expect me to argue for Saddam Hussein? Oh, this is ridiculous, you're purposefully / misremembering!

(A mobile phone rings once. Both look vaguely to it. Pause.)

—Now I'm wondering what *else* I've said to you that you're unclear on.

CRAIG

What does *that* mean.

KELLY

I'm wondering about our having a *baby* . . .

(Pause.)

CRAIG

What about it.

KELLY

I don't know! I thought we were / clear about—

CRAIG

We just talked about it tonight—when I get back, when I finish / school—

KELLY

In front of *Peter.*

CRAIG

What . . .

KELLY

—*Peter* brought it up, *Peter* asked if we were going to have a baby—were you saying it just to please him?

CRAIG

Kelly, we've talked about this a hundred times—I want to wait till I'm teaching, I don't want to take any more money from your father.

KELLY

I still don't see what the big deal is—

CRAIG

The big deal is, he's a *cock.*

(Pause.)

—Jesus! We talked about starting a family—sitting right on this couch, looking out at the *cloud of death* hanging over / the city—

KELLY

—Please, please don't invoke / that—

CRAIG

Why not? That day is seared into my—every single thing we said to one / another!

KELLY

—You know what? I'm tired, I want to go to sleep. I'll sleep on the couch— *(Goes to couch)* Go sleep with your brother.

CRAIG

—Oh, fuck you!

(Craig gets his keys, moves to the apartment door.)

KELLY

Where are you going?

CRAIG

For a walk.

KELLY

Craig—

(Craig opens the door.)

Craig—don't go—

(Craig stops. Pause.
Kelly approaches him. He shuts the door. Turns. Pause.
Kelly leans in, kisses Craig. Pause. He kisses back. The kiss grows . . .
A mobile phone rings once. Craig looks at it. Kelly keeps kissing him.
Craig detaches himself and goes to the mobile phone, picks it up. Pause.)

—What?

CRAIG

(Reads phone message) "Did Tim leave yet. Horny."

(Craig looks up at Kelly.)

"Adam."

(Pause.)

KELLY

—You don't know what it means. It could just be a—like a joke or something.

CRAIG

A *joke?*

KELLY

Like he teases him by sending him texts like that.

(Pause.)

What.

(Pause.)

What.

(Craig looks at the phone again a moment, then puts it down. He gets up, goes to the kitchen, opens a cabinet, a drawer . . .)

What are you—

(Craig grabs a pot and a spoon, goes into the bedroom, off. Kelly stands. Offstage sounds of the spoon hitting the pot, loudly. After some time Peter comes out of the bedroom. Stumbles. Sees Kelly, smiles.)

PETER

Hey . . . sorry . . .

(Peter grabs his jacket, starts to go. Kelly sees his phone.)

KELLY

—Don't forget your phone—I think someone might have texted you while you were asleep.

PETER

—Oh.

(Pause. Kelly goes into the bedroom, off. Peter takes the phone from his pocket, checks it. Then goes out the door, off.
Pause.
The bedroom door opens. Craig comes out, goes to the couch, curls into it. Grips himself tight.
Pause. Kelly follows.)

KELLY

Craig.

(Pause.)

Craig, what's happening.

(She moves to Craig. He curls more tightly into himself, burrows deeper into the couch. Kelly turns and goes back into the bedroom, off.)

5.

Kelly watches TV. Peter comes out of the bedroom.

PETER

Jon Stewart!

KELLY

(Turns) My other TiVo favorite.

PETER

Yeah, he's funny. But it's weird—I was at a party a couple nights ago? And this guy starts saying Bush is as bad as Hitler. *Then* he starts talking about how hilarious *The Daily Show* is. And I thought—if you were in Germany in the 1930s, would you watch a show where some smartass made fun of Hitler? Little mustache jokes while he's throwing Jews in the ovens? I mean if you really think George Bush is evil, then how can you laugh at "George Bush is dumb" jokes?

KELLY

It's the sensibility. The sensibility comes closer to conveying the truth than the real news does, I think that's what people respond to.

PETER

Yeah, but whose truth is being conveyed? Jon Stewart has so much privilege, I think it's a pretty small slice of the "truth" he's conveying. Like when I watch him make fun of evangelicals—if you really care about the truth, you can't just speak to your own tiny group, you have to figure out how to speak to the community.

KELLY

The community . . . ?

PETER

People who may not be like you but that you still have—something in common with. A basic humanity. Even if they *do* believe in God, or believe in the war in Iraq. Go to the Indiana State Fair—those are the people we need to figure out how to talk to. They're not going away, we can't just make fun of them. Don't you think?

KELLY

But aren't they beyond reach? These people think the Rapture is coming. They think people like us are going to burn in hell—literally.

PETER

But that's the—that was one thing about Craig. He could talk to those Army guys like—it didn't matter, Harvard, all the books he read—he never forgot where he came from. He knew that these people, whatever insane things they believed—he thought you could reach into the core of them, and find something deeper and truer than all the surface stuff, God and politics and all that.

KELLY

I don't know—God and politics go pretty deep.

PETER

(Mostly conceding) Yes and no . . .

KELLY

He thought we could reach the Iraqis too. Do you think he was right about that?

(Pause.)

PETER

I hear you. I just don't want to write people off, I guess. —I mean, how do you feel as a therapist? Someone comes to you with all these problems, doing all these bad things to themselves, to other people . . . you have to believe that there's a way to reach them, right? No matter how awful or crazy they seem . . .

(Pause.)

KELLY

No, I agree . . . —What did your director say, is everything okay?

PETER

—I chickened out, I still haven't called him. I was just leaving messages for my agents, and my manager, and my lawyer.

KELLY

—Your publicist is out of town?

PETER

I really should have gone to the stage manager.

KELLY

I think you're the last person who needs to be questioning his actions tonight—

PETER

I've kind of been—I don't know . . . Scott—the director—on opening night . . . —Tim had left the party, he doesn't like staying out late—and I was really drunk, and Tim doesn't have much of a sex drive because of the Paxil and—I ended up following Scott into the bathroom—and—Drew, my understudy—came into the bathroom and saw—Scott blowing me basically. So . . . —I'm sure word got around to the company, I'm sure John heard . . .

KELLY

—Oh.

(Pause.)

PETER

And—I might as well just put it all out there—I've been sleeping with Adam still. —So basically, that's my life.

(Pause.)

You're moving, aren't you.

(Pause. Kelly turns off the TV. She looks at Peter, nods.)

When.

KELLY

Next week.

PETER

Next *week*. Where?

KELLY

I have a good friend from school, in Ann Arbor. She's just been through a divorce. I'm going to go up there for a while.

PETER

What about your practice?

KELLY

I referred everyone.

(Pause.)

PETER

Why couldn't you . . . did I *do* something that made you not want to talk to me, / or—

KELLY

It's just me. I haven't wanted contact with anybody.

(Pause.)

I didn't know you were in this much pain, Peter. I'm sorry.

PETER

Oh, it's all—drama, I'm fine, really. I'm so sorry *you've* been— I mean I figured things were tough, that's why you hadn't . . . —I think I had the idea because, just, being in the play made me—I had all these hopes going into it, but it turned out to be like *Long Day's Journey to the Hamptons*—actors constantly checking messages, luxurious spreads of pastries at every rehearsal, Scott taking up all this time telling stories about which Hollywood actors have big dicks—I wanted to scream! The play is like being in a *war,* these people are trying to kill each other— literally! My father won't spend money on treatment for my TB, for the sanitarium! And no one was taking it seriously . . . So I sort of —would retreat into my own little world, and read Craig's emails . . . they were so inspiring, I mean, just—this extraordinary thing of him turning against the war, you know? And I kept thinking of the two of you, how much you had wanted a / child—

KELLY

—Turning against the war?

PETER

Yeah—did you—I was wondering if that was something he could even talk about—

KELLY

Not—there were limits to what he could say, he / wasn't—

PETER

So you had no— Oh, Kelly—reading the emails is like—this *awakening,* it's like the birth of this whole other person! I know you said you're not ready—but if you ever do want to read them—just—please—anytime . . .

KELLY

Thank you—I might some day.

(Pause. Peter smiles at Kelly. Looks away.)

PETER

—It's late, I should get going. Big day tomorrow, God only / knows—

KELLY

Are you—where are / you—

(Peter goes to his bag.)

PETER

—If you have email in Ann Arbor, I really would like to stay in / touch—

KELLY

—It's late, stay here.

(Kelly looks at Peter. Pause.)

PETER

—Okay!

KELLY

—Take the bedroom. In the morning I'll make some pancakes.

PETER

Eeek, pancakes.

KELLY

—Oh, right. What can you—I can make them without / sugar—

PETER

Ah, fuck it—pancakes! With *gobs* of maple syrup—

(They laugh. Pause.)

I'm—glad we could be honest with each other.

KELLY

Me, too.

PETER

Yeah. —Just—gonna use the bathroom . . .

(Peter goes into the bathroom, off. Kelly takes the bedsheet off the box and goes to the couch. Sees Peter's bag. Goes to it, unzips it, looks in. Begins to reach in. Toilet flushes. Kelly zips up the bag, moves away. Peter comes out of the bathroom, takes his bag.)

You know—I really don't mind sleeping on the couch . . .

KELLY

Please—take the bedroom.

PETER

You sure?

KELLY

I'm sure.

PETER

Okay. —G'night.

(Peter moves toward the bedroom.)

KELLY

Can I . . . —

(Peter turns.)

I think part of my hesitation with—the emails, your asking if you could share them with me before—I think because they were written to *you* I feel—that it's really not / my—

PETER

—Oh, no, I'm *sure* Craig would have wanted me to share them with you.

(Pause.)

KELLY

Then I think I—I would like to / read them if it's—

PETER

Oh, of course, absolutely. *(Opens his bag)* There's one in partic-ular I've most wanted you to . . . *(Picks one)* I *think* this is the—they all blur together a little . . .

(Peter sits down, as if to begin reading. Kelly does not move to sit.)

KELLY

—Oh.

PETER

Is it okay if I read it to you?

KELLY

It's not—I can read it.

PETER

Oh, you'd rather . . . I just thought it would be—I guess I'm so eager to *share* . . .

(Pause.)

KELLY

If you'd—sure.

PETER

Is that okay?

KELLY

—Sure.

(Kelly sits.)

PETER

Okay. If it gets to be too much or anything—just tell me, I'll stop.

(Pause. He reads:)

"Abu Ghraib is already a punch line; I'll spare you the jokes. For about five minutes we all felt the truth of it but that feeling got swept away in the hot desert wind like every other emotion here." —A little Faulknerian. "From what I can tell, it's not a big deal at home either. I think the images are a real comfort to people—that we're the powerful ones, in control, alive, clothed.

66

I had a memory the other night of the time Dad put his fist through the car windshield. Do you remember? I recall so vividly Mom telling us when she was taking us to school the next day that it was a Vietnam flashback. We couldn't have been older than six. We were coming back from dinner, Dad was driving, Mom was saying something to him—and suddenly there was a crunch. I looked up and the windshield was like a spiderweb, and there was Dad's bleeding fist, gripping the steering wheel tight . . . I looked over at Mom and I remember thinking that she was going to look a certain way, upset or scared . . . but instead I saw her grinning. A little creeping grin on her face. You were looking out the window like you hadn't noticed anything, so I punched you in the arm. You said, 'Ow,' and Dad looked back for a second, then turned back to the road. I think I've remembered this now, after so many years, because what I learned in that instant—that to be married to a man so powerful he could put his fist through glass was what made our mother smile—is exactly how I feel here: so powerful I can't stop smiling, while suffering a wound I do not feel."

(Pause. Peter looks up.)

KELLY

—Jesus.

PETER

No memory.

KELLY

—You don't remember that at all?

PETER

Vague memory of Craig hitting me and Dad not doing anything. But that happened all the time.

KELLY

—Craig would hit you?

PETER

It was weird. When Dad would hit me, Craig would yell at him to stop. But then Craig would hit me a lot too. When I would go tell Dad, he wouldn't do anything. And when I would go tell Mom she would say, "Go tell your father."

(Pause.)

KELLY

I'm sorry.

PETER

Oh, you know, everyone has a childhood. —Craig told me once—your dad abused you?

KELLY

Emotionally.

PETER

He was never really specific . . .

KELLY

Neither was my father.

PETER

You mean . . .

KELLY

He wasn't around, he was having affairs, he bought me lots of things I didn't want . . . my mother was on too much Valium to care.

PETER

I'm sorry.

(Kelly nods. Pause.)

Is this okay? Should I / keep—

PETER

KELLY

Please.

PETER

It's very eloquent, isn't it?

KELLY

It's beautiful.

PETER

A bit purple here and there . . .

(Peter looks back at the paper, reads:)

"The malaise among the men has taken a turn. It's clear to everyone now that we are not equipped to bring this country back to life. The city is dying and we are the ones killing it. But I do not blame my men. They were told they would be heroes bringing freedom, and instead have been told to invade people's homes and take their freedom. They are ordered to protect themselves from violence by actively doing violence, which leads to more violence to protect themselves against: no sane person could survive these tasks. I have begun to wonder if I myself will recover from who I have become here, in just a few short months. But then in quieter moments I find myself thrown back into memories of who I was before and am faced with the realization that the horror I feel here is not—" Hmmm.

(Pause.)

This sort of goes on for a while, there was a part at the end—

KELLY

No, please, keep reading.

PETER

—Reading out loud it's longer than I . . . there's a, where is the /
part—

KELLY

—Go back, what was he saying about the "horror"—"the realization that the horror I feel here"—I want to hear that.

(Pause. Peter looks at the paper.)

PETER

"But then in quieter moments I find myself thrown back into
memories of who I was before and am faced with the realization
that the horror I feel here is not . . . something I fully understand
. . . It is unclear which way the narrative of this war will twist
next. Faulkner understood that the psychological legacy of war
is that / the individual—"

KELLY

—Are you skipping something?

PETER

No. No.

KELLY

The—read it again?

(Pause.)

PETER

I think—that part might have been something he meant just for
me, actually.

(Pause.)

KELLY

What are you skipping?

PETER

It's not really—

(Kelly takes the email from Peter and reads it. She looks up. Pause.)

I think he—I think he meant just fantasies, or—

KELLY

"Fantasies"?

PETER

He says "need," need's not—I mean Fort Benning was probably anxiety, but—

KELLY

(Reads) "—in quieter moments I find myself thrown back into memories of who I was before and am faced with the realization that the horror I feel here is not just a consequence of the war, but is horror of the core of me, of who I have always been. In fact I have felt more clearheaded here than ever before. I haven't felt the overwhelming need to sexually demean women that has haunted me my entire life, and haven't fucked since leaving Fort Benning."

(She puts down the email.)

Every night I let him fuck me—every night of my / life!

PETER

—I don't—I don't think / he's saying—

KELLY

—Did you know he fucked other women.

(Long pause.)

PETER

One time—

KELLY

—I knew it—

PETER

we were—do you want me / to—

KELLY

Yes.

PETER

—We were in a bar, we were drunk, he went to the bathroom—
he was gone a while, so when he came back I just said, "Are you
okay." Like maybe he was throwing up . . .

(Pause.)

He said, "I think the bitch bit me."

(Pause.)

KELLY

"I think the bitch bit me."

PETER

I just thought he / was joking—

KELLY

—I knew when he wouldn't apply for a deferment. I knew—

PETER

—I think it's like, it's the violence just finally got to him, you
know? / The—

KELLY

It has nothing to do with, no—he said, it's who he's *always* been—

PETER

No, that's what I mean—like—five years old, Dad took us shooting, there's photo albums of dead animals / all—

KELLY

Don't blame this on your father, it's / not—

PETER

He loved you so much, Kelly—

KELLY

—He was a coward!

PETER

—He fucking shot his head off, right? He obviously felt guilty!

KELLY

Guilt? Over *me*? No, that's not guilt, / no—

PETER

What is it then?

KELLY

—He wanted to get *away* from me!

PETER

—What?

KELLY

He wanted to get away from / me!

PETER

No—

KELLY

so he went to Iraq and *shot himself*—*oh*!

(Kelly rises.)

Leave my house I need to be alone—

PETER

—Kelly—

(Kelly goes into bedroom, off. Peter stays seated.)

6.

Craig is on the couch. Near dawn. Kelly opens the bedroom door, comes out a few steps.

CRAIG

Hey.

KELLY

You're talking.

(Pause.)

CRAIG

I have to leave / in a—

KELLY

I know what time it is.

(Pause. Kelly comes to the couch, sits.)

CRAIG

Get any sleep?

(Kelly shakes her head no. Craig smiles.)

Thinking about fucked-her-so-hard-she?

(Pause.)

KELLY

Why would I be thinking about him.

CRAIG

You're seeing him.

(Pause.)

KELLY

No. I am not thinking / about—

CRAIG

Call the bluff.

KELLY

—What?

CRAIG

Tell him you know what he's doing. Every time you listen to him go on about one of these women he's getting / off on it—

KELLY

You have never met him. Yes, he is exasperating. But he is a human being, with a history, who is in pain—who is communicating his / pain

CRAIG

He's *acting* like he's in pain—

KELLY

in the only way he knows. He's trying to make me feel small, so I can know how *he* feels: small.

CRAIG

No, he's just trying to make you feel small. And he'll keep doing it until you crack, and then he'll leave.

KELLY

—We have very different views of human nature.

(Pause.)

Do you love me, Craig?

(Pause.)

CRAIG

I don't think we should have a serious discussion right now.

KELLY

Why not.

CRAIG

I'm not capable of it. I'm stressed—

KELLY

Things have come up tonight. We can't / just—

CRAIG

I think saying anything is a bad idea.

KELLY

—I think you should be able to answer the question.

(Pause.)

Do you love me.

(Pause.)

Did you?

CRAIG

Did I what.

KELLY

Did you ever love me.

(Pause.)

CRAIG

Of course.

KELLY

Of course?

CRAIG

Of course I loved you.

KELLY

Loved?

(Pause.)

When did you stop.

(Pause.)

When did / you—

CRAIG

After we got married. I knew it was a mistake. I knew I didn't love you.

(Pause. Kelly cries. She punches Craig repeatedly. She stops. Pause.)

I have to get dressed.

(Pause. Craig goes into the bedroom, off. Kelly hyperventilates. Calms some. She picks up her phone, goes to her phone book, dials.)

KELLY

Hi, this is a message for Bradley. It's Kelly Conners calling. I'm sorry to be calling so early and with such short notice. I need to cancel this morning's session. I'm very sorry. I'll see you at our regular time next week. Take care.

7.

Peter is on the couch asleep, a script open before him. The bed-room door opens, Kelly comes out. Pause. She looks at Peter. Goes into the kitchen and runs water, opens cabinets, makes noise. Peter wakes up. Sees Kelly. She sees him.

PETER

Sorry . . .

(Kelly makes tea. Peter looks at the box of books.)

I was looking over one of my speeches—"It was a great mistake, my being born a man"—I got inspired by all of Craig's books. I must have passed out . . . Melville, Hawthorne, Hemingway, Faulkner . . . I remember in high school Craig was reading *A Farewell to Arms*. He said it was a war novel—I thought it was about a double amputee . . . God, America had so many great writers . . .

(Kelly continues making tea.)

—Oh, shit, what time is it?

KELLY

—Nine.

PETER

Phew—I have a company meeting at ten. Spoke to Scott—told him what happened, he talked to John, John I guess feels terrible . . . Sounds like we'll all kiss and make up.

(Pause. Peter looks at Kelly.)

I'm sure this won't make—much of a difference to you, but—I'm really sorry about what happened last night.

KELLY

—Thank you, I accept your apology.

(Kelly straightens things up in the kitchen. Peter looks at the couch.)

PETER

—I'm gonna miss this couch! I remember, on 9/11—I had just moved to L.A., and I remember calling here, all day, I couldn't get through till late in the night—Craig picked up the phone, and I remember this peace in his voice—telling me about how you two just sat on the couch all day—looking out the window, at the cloud, holding each other . . . When I think of 9/11, that's always the picture I have . . .

(Kelly does not respond.)

—*That's* what I forgot to ask you! Whatever happened to fucked-her-so-hard-she?

KELLY

—He stopped coming.

PETER

Why?

KELLY

I had to cancel a session, and he never came again.

PETER

Huh. I had this whole fantasy that he was why you changed your numbers, like he was stalking you / or something—

(Kelly stops.)

KELLY

I changed my numbers because of you.

(Pause.)

PETER

Because of *me*?

KELLY

Peter, you've invaded my home, no warning, you come in here, you / read me

PETER

I didn't have your numbers—

KELLY

this email—say what you will, you did it. So please—just say good-bye, and leave.

(Pause.)

PETER

When did you change them, after getting my letter?

KELLY

I just want to start over.

PETER

I don't understand, what did I do?

KELLY

I just told you: I wanted to start over.

PETER

But—there was no one I could talk to about him, you were / the—

KELLY

There are therapists.

PETER

But—I love you.

(Pause.)

KELLY

Bye.

(Pause.)

PETER

Fine.

(He grabs his bag, starts to go, then stops.)

—For you.

(He puts the emails down on the couch.)

KELLY

—How *dare* you—*no!*

(Peter goes, off. Pause.
 Kelly turns to the window. The sun is shining, sounds of the city coming to life. She looks out the window. Craig comes out of the bedroom, in uniform, with luggage.)

CRAIG

It's time for me to go.

(Kelly turns. Pause. Craig goes to the couch and sits. He cries. Kelly goes to the couch and sits. After a time:)

KELLY

Listen. I think you were right. I think this stress is—it was a mistake to talk. I don't think this is who we really / are—

CRAIG

I have to go, I / can't—

KELLY

I know you do. We'll talk when—phone, email, whatever you're most comfortable with, whenever you—we'll find a way to understand what's / happening—

CRAIG

I don't—I don't think that's a good idea.

(Pause.)

KELLY

What's not.

CRAIG

Being in touch.

KELLY

Being in touch . . . at all?

(Pause.)

CRAIG

I have to go.

KELLY

Craig—

(Craig rises. He gathers his things and goes to the door.)

CRAIG

Good-bye.

(Pause. Craig goes, off.

After a time, Kelly gets up and pours herself a cup of tea. She returns to the couch, turns on the TV. Puts on The Daily Show. *A moment passes. She looks at the emails sitting on the couch. Pause. She picks up one, begins to read.*

She stops, puts it down. Pause.

She goes to the box of books, opens it. Goes to the emails, picks them up. Places them in the box. She sits. Begins placing books neatly into the box.

On the TV, sounds of Jon Stewart, laughter, applause . . .)

END OF PLAY

CHRISTOPHER SHINN was born in Hartford and lives in New York. His plays have premiered in London at the Royal Court Theatre and the Soho Theatre, and in the U.S. at Lincoln Center Theater, Manhattan Theatre Club, Playwrights Horizons, the Vineyard Theatre and South Coast Repertory. He is the recipient of an OBIE Award in playwriting and a Guggenheim Fellowship. He teaches playwriting at the New School.